AF434742

Latter-day Grooks
3

From the Words and Wisdom of
Dieter F. Uchtdorf

Bill Wylson

First Edition published May 2023
Second Edition published October 2024

Green Stem Media
White Horse Books
South Jordan, Utah 84009

*"If your life is a leaf
That the seasons tear off and condemn,
[He] will bind you with love
That is graceful and green as a stem."*
L. Cohen

www.billwylsonbooks.com
www.greenstemmedia.com

Table of Contents

An Introduction to Grooks

Grooks were initially created by the Danish poet Piet Hein (1905–1996), who wrote over 10,000 of them in both Danish and English. Hein was a polymath (designer, mathematician, inventor, author, and poet), often writing under the pseudonym Kumbel, which means 'tombstone.'

A grook ('gruk' in Danish) is a short aphoristic poem or rhyming aphorism. An aphorism is a concise, terse, laconic, or memorable expression of a general truth or principle. Aphorisms are often handed down by tradition from generation to generation. Literary experts suggest that the term 'gruk' is a compilation of the Danish words' GRin and sUK,' meaning to laugh and sigh, but Piet Hein said he felt that the term came to him out of thin air.

Aphoristic collections, known as wisdom literature, are prominent in Western civilization. They have had a profound impact on the canons of ancient societies, such as the works of the sutra literature of Hinduism and Buddhism, the Biblical Ecclesiastes, Islamic hadiths, the golden verses of Pythagoras, Hesiod's Works and Days, the Delphic maxims, and Epictetus' Handbook. A 1559 oil–on–oak-panel painting, Netherlandish Proverbs (also called The Blue Cloak or The Topsy Turvy World) by Pieter Bruegel, the Elder, artfully depicts a land populated with literal renditions of Flemish aphorisms of the day.

Hein's short poems, or gruks, first appeared in the daily newspaper Politiken in April 1940. Many have tried to define what a grook essentially is. Most grooks say what we may think ourselves. Still, they put pertinent new perspectives on everyday observations, presenting the reader with small instructions on the art of living.

His grooks were meant to be a spirit-building, coded form of passive resistance. The grooks are multi-faceted and characterized by irony, paradox, brevity, precise use of language, rhythm, and rhyme. They were often satiric.

Hein, a descendant of Piet Pieterszoon Hein, the 17th-century Dutch naval hero, was born in Copenhagen, Denmark. He studied at the Institute for Theoretical Physics of the University of Copenhagen (later to become the Niels Bohr Institute) and the Technical University of Denmark. Yale awarded him an honorary doctorate in 1972.

Piet Hein was married four times and had five sons from his last three marriages. He died in his home in Funen, Denmark, in 1996.

One of the author's favorite Piet Hein grooks is entitled:

To Sum Up

It may be observed, in a general way,
that life would be better, distinctly,
If more of the people with nothing to say
were able to say it succinctly.

In this volume, the author has attempted to cite the words and teachings of Elder Dieter F. Uchtdorf, an apostle of the Church of Jesus Christ of Latter-day Saints, and to express his ideas as latter-day grooks.

Message from the Author

The Latter-day Saints have a unique form of wisdom literature primarily unfamiliar to the world. It is the writings of Latter-day prophets and apostles. It is often easier to recall essential writings when they appear in poetic form because poetry resonates with us. We enjoy reading or hearing something that reflects our minds or hearts.

As Elder Uchtdorf suggests, "For members of the Church, education is not merely a good idea—it's a commandment. We are to learn *'of things both in heaven and in the earth, and under the earth; things which have been, things which are, things which must shortly come to pass; things which are at home, things which are abroad.'"* D&C 88:79,80

I sincerely pray that these messages of Elder Uchtdorf will be written onto the walls of our hearts and minds and offer us hope, strength, and encouragement in our effort to resist evil and overcome the world.

"Keep thy father's commandment, and forsake not the law of thy mother:

"Bind them continually upon thine heart, and tie them about thy neck.

"When thou goest, it shall lead thee; when thou sleepest, it shall keep thee; and when thou awakest, it shall talk with thee."

Proverbs 6:20-22.

The Great Commandment

*"Love is the measure of our faith, the
inspiration for our obedience, and the true
altitude of our discipleship."*

Don't you see?
Love should be
our walk
and our talk.

Try (And Keep on Trying)

Just keep at it
until the difficult
becomes possible,
and the possible
becomes habit.

I am grateful for

Gratitude

Brothers and Sisters,
here's a thought:

We can choose to be grateful,
no matter what.

A Step Forward

Straighten your back—
Roll up your sleeve—
Take a step forward—

He still expects us to believe,

even if it's hard to do so,

that is how we learn
        and grow.

No Respecter of Persons

Privileged or disadvantaged,
rich or poor,
great or small,

His light is available
to us all.

It Matters Not

It matters not
how ruined your life,
how deep your bitterness,
how scarlet your sin,

those without hope,
who suffer in strife—
surrender to God,
let the healing begin.

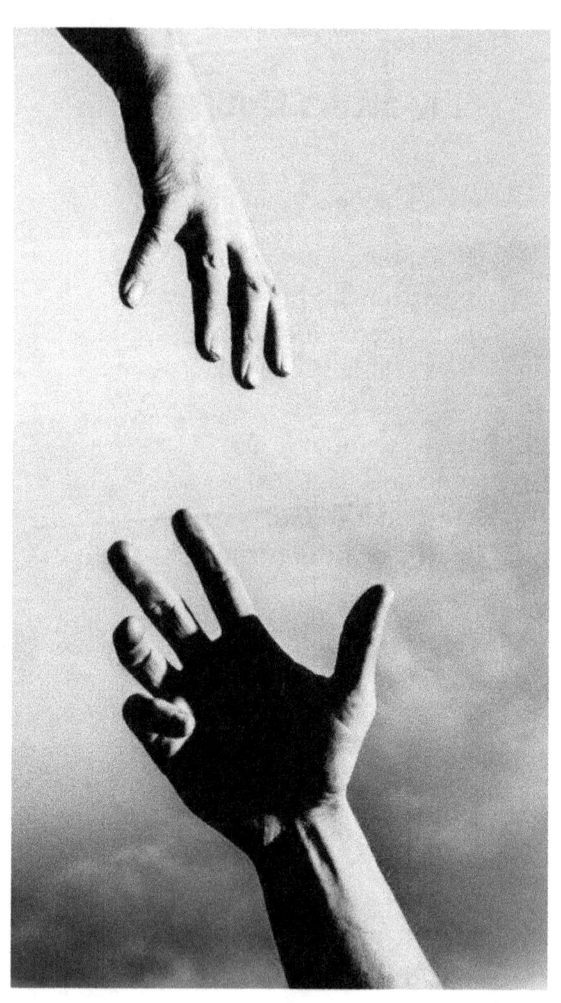

God Calls to You

It's no great mystery—
no matter your history,

if you have faltered,
failed,
feel broken,
bitter,
betrayed,
beaten,
or blue—

the Savior extends
His hand to you.

Listen

To the humble
and the meek:

If you will hear Him,
He will speak.

Start Where You Are

God will take you as you are
at this very moment and start

to work with your desire,
your trust, and your willing heart.

Stand Loyal

Do we just
talk the talk,
        or do we
        enthusiastically
walk the walk?

A Tribute to Joseph

God didn't wait for a person
with a perfect five-star rating
to restore His gospel. If He had,
well, He'd still be waiting.

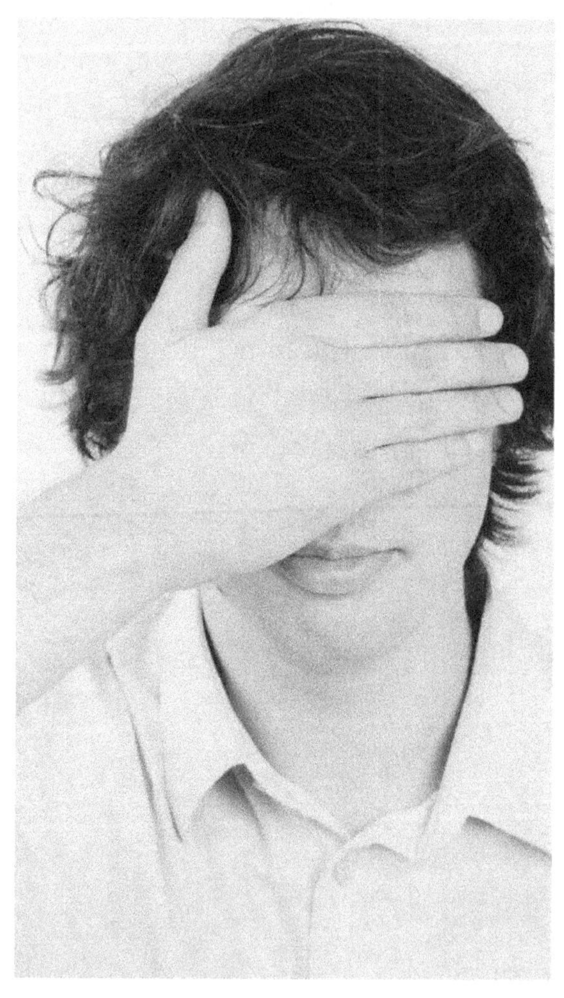

One Simple Fact:

40

Our faith is not blind.

We believe in God
because of things we *know*

with our heart and mind,

and not because of things
we do not know.

KEEP
it
SIMPLE

Curing *Weltschmerz*

Discipleship begins,
it is true,
with three simple words:

Believe, love, and do.

Nearer My God to Thee

You don't have
to be perfect,
per sé,

just develop your faith,
and draw nearer to Him
each day.

What Hope?

The human plight
is a sad, sad song;

we assume we are right
even when we are wrong.

Draw Near to God

Belief is not a painting
we look at and admire.

It is a plow

we take into the fields
to make furrows for seeds

by the sweat of our brow.

GOD
loves
YOU

This Very Day and Always

50

God is not waiting to love you
until all your bad habits
    and sins go away.

He loves you today.

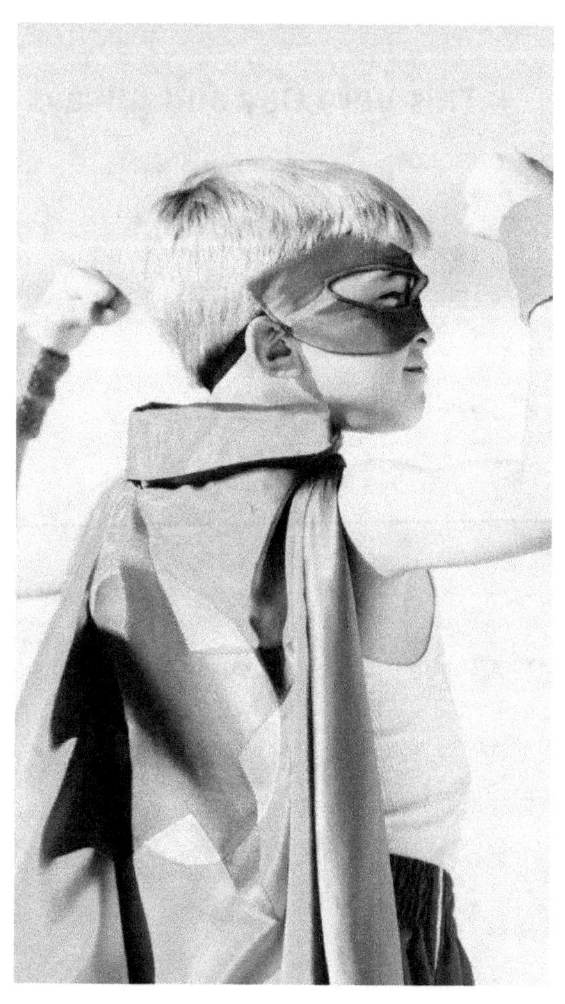

Testimony to His Power

As a testimony of His power
(and not of mankind's services)

God uses the weak and plain
to bring about His purposes.

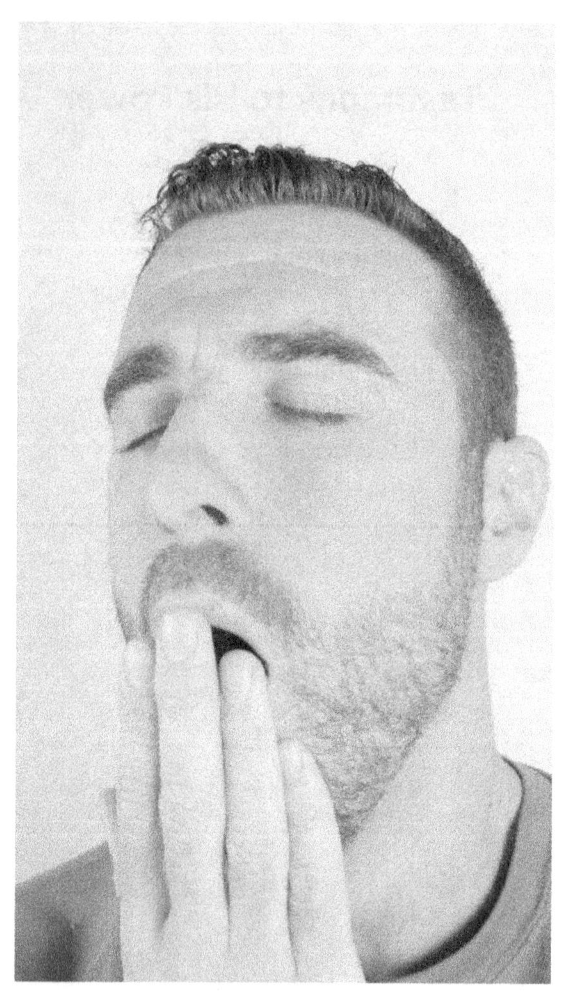

Awaken

A once-a-week
or once-a-day
discipleship
is not your call.

Yours is an effort
wholeheartedly made
of once
and for all.

The Words of the Prophets

When we stray—
or fall away

their words tell us how

to get back
on track.

Y
OU
CAN

Turn Your Heart

True heartfelt repentance
brings with it this vow
of heavenly assurance:

"You can do it now."

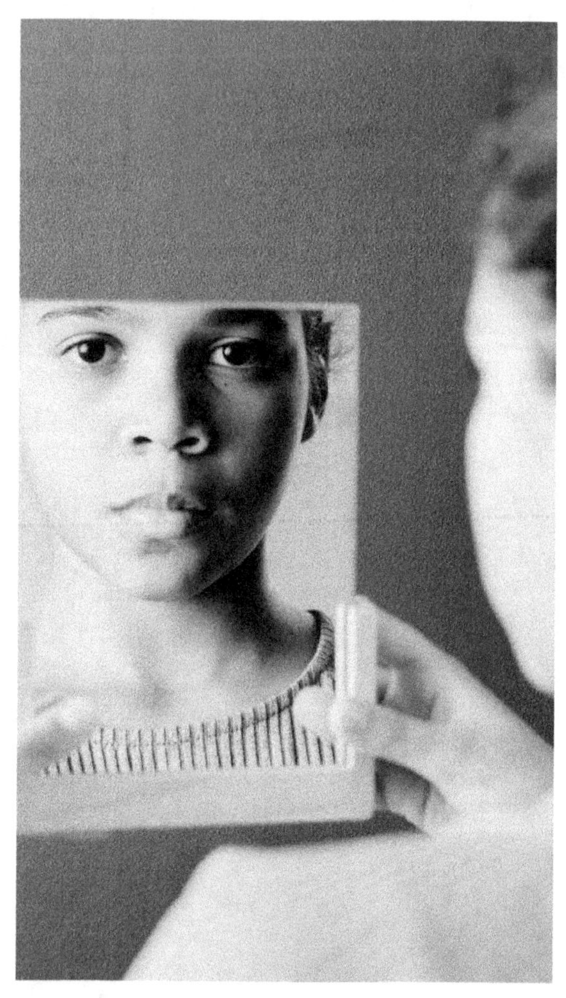

Footnote

Of all the people in the world,
(this fact couldn't be any clearer)

the one who's the hardest to forgive
is the one looking back in the mirror.

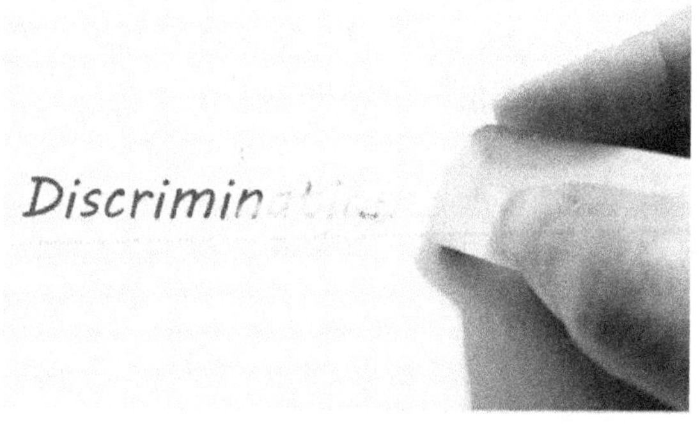

Discrimin

Endless Compassion

Looking through
the lens of love
of God's only
begotten Son,

we cannot discount,
        disregard, or
        discriminate

against anyone.

A Paradox of Man:

Compared to God,
man is nothing;

and yet, how odd,

that we are
everything to God.

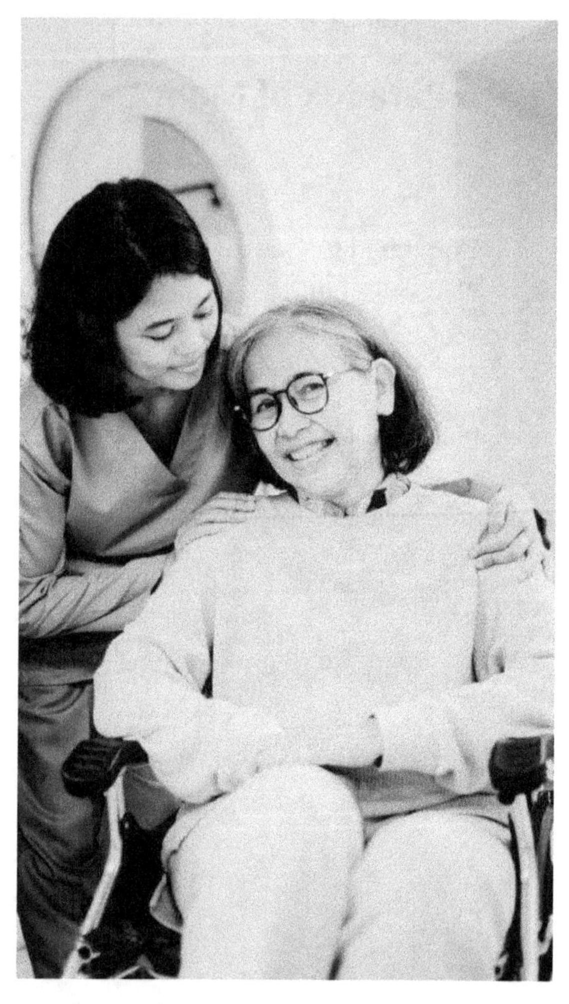

Our Part

Our part is:

to love and serve
God and then,

to love and serve
God's children.

Eternal Repercussions

Life is short,
so, remember this rhyme:

Regrets can last
an awfully long time.

Charity's Great Enemy

Set aside
your pride.

Imperfect People

We are a welcoming,
loving,
kind,
sincere,
hardworking,
and even heroic sect.

And we are also

painfully imperfect.

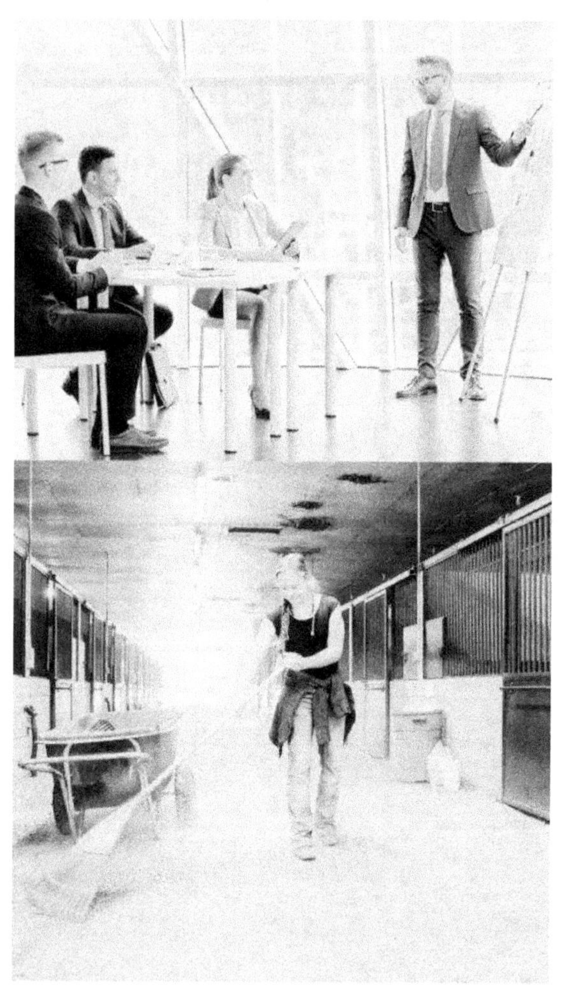

The First Shall Be Last

The Lord doesn't care at all
if we work in a marble hall

or labor in a stable stall.
He knows and loves us all.

Distractions

"We cannot and we must not allow ourselves to get distracted from our sacred duty. We cannot and we must not lose focus on the things that matter most."

Remember,
in your life-long
pursuit for success,

it is possible
to take even
good things to excess.

Day of Judgment

That will be a day
of love and mercy,
when heavy hearts grow light,

when tears of gratitude
replace tears of grief,
when all, at last, will be right.

Lessons in Adversity

We learn critical lessons
in the trial of adversity
that form our character
and shape our destiny.

Regardless

Regardless of our differences,
we seek to embrace one another

as sons and daughters of
our beloved Heavenly Father.

Take Up Thy Bed, and Walk

Even the deepest spiritual wounds
—yes, those that appear
unendurable—

through the healing power
of Jesus Christ, even *those* wounds
can be curable.

Learn

*"Learn of things both in heaven and in the
earth, and under the earth; things which
have been, things which are, things which
must shortly come to pass; things which are
at home, things which are abroad."*

Education is not merely
a good idea and investment—
for members of the church
it is a commandment.

Because of Him

*"Jesus Christ, the Son of God, died so that
our mistakes might not condemn us and
forever halt our progress."*

The mistakes we carry
in our inventory

can become stepping-stones
to greater glory.

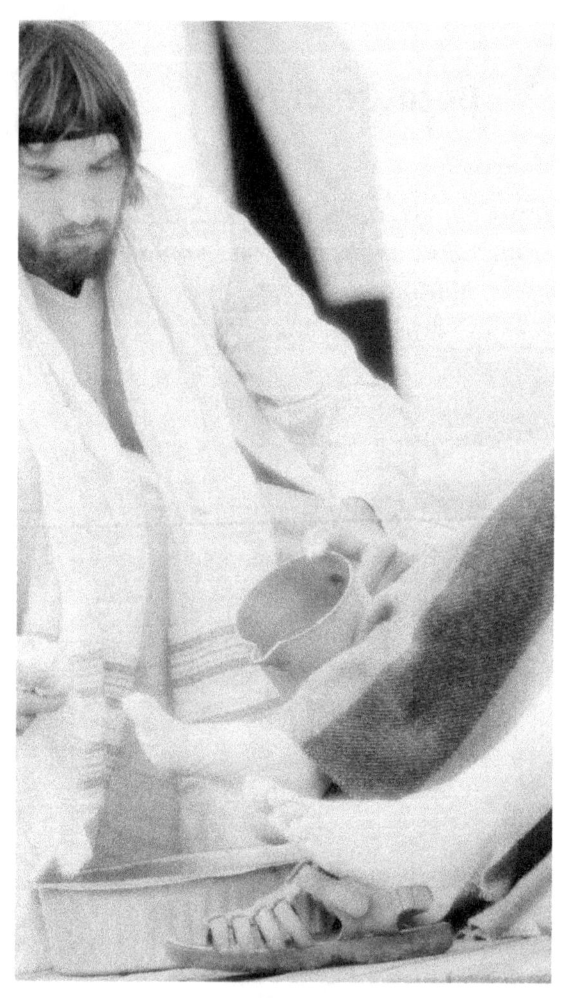

Humility

Those who are humble in this life
(this comes from sacred text),

will surely wear crowns of glory
when they go into the next.

Spiritual Healing

Step away from
the shadows of the world,
step away from the eternal night.

You will find hope and
spiritual healing
in Christ's everlasting light.

A Fundamental Truth

As we lift others
from the mire,

we'll find ourselves
a little higher.

Pro Tanto Quid
Retribuamus

Consider the question:
What shall we give
in return for so much?

What shall we give
for the flood of truth
God has poured out on us?

God Is on Our Side

God is not
angry, vengeful, or
retaliatory.

His purpose is
to exalt us;
that is His work
and His glory.

Once Upon A Time...

Opposition in All Things

"In stories, as in life, adversity teaches us things we cannot learn otherwise."

Sandwiched between
"once upon a time" and "ever after,
happily"

we all experience, in our own way,
our fair share of adversity.

WHERE?
WHEN? WHY?
WHO? WHERE? WHAT? HOW?
WHAT? HOW? WHY?
WHEN? WHY?
WHO? WHEN?
WHAT?
WHERE?
WHEN?
HOW? HOW?
WHEN?
WHERE? WHICH? WHOSE? WHEN? WHY?
WHICH?
WHOSE?
HOW
WHAT? HOW?
WHO? WHERE? WHAT?
WHY? HOW
WHAT? HOW? WHY?
WHO? WHERE? WHAT? HOW?
WHERE? WHICH? WHOSE? WHEN? WHY?
WHAT?
WHAT?
WHY? HOW? WHERE?
WHO? WHOSE?
WHERE? WHAT? HOW?
WHY?
HOW?
WHERE?
WHO?
WHERE? WHAT? HOW?
WHERE? WHICH? WHOSE? WHEN? WHY?
HOW? WHERE? WHY?
WHERE?
HOW?
HOW? WHO?
WHO? WHERE? WHAT? HOW?
WHAT? HOW? WHY?
WHERE?
WHAT?
HOW?
HOW?
WHAT?
WHAT? WHERE? HOW?

We Have Answers!

The restored gospel
of the Lord, Jesus Christ,
answers the most complex
questions in life.

The Important Lessons of Life

By learning from our mistakes
and repenting of our nastiness,

we can realize for ourselves,
"wickedness never was happiness."

You Matter

At times you may feel
insignificant, invisible,
alone, forgotten, and grim.

But always remember,
my brothers and sisters—
you matter to Him!

What Faith Is

People fail to understand—

there are more ways to see
than with the eye,

more ways to hear
than with the ear,

more ways to feel
than with the hand.

Perfect Love

Everything He does—
every blessing He gives

and every blessing He withholds—
is for *our* eternal bliss.

Dosing Off

Church sleep is,
I'm sure you'll recall,

among the healthiest
sleeps of all.

On the Road Again

Dear friends,
don't wait too long
on your road to Damascus.

Move forward in
faith, hope, and charity,
just like He has asked us.

Harriet

After two young missionaries
led Harriet's family
to enter the baptismal gate,

a young Deacon named Dieter
thought to himself:
"These missionaries are doing
great!"

Harken

To better hear
His voice,

turn down the volume
of worldly noise.

Advice From A Friend

"When we 'inhale' the praise of others, that praise will be our compensation."

When people treat you kindly,
offering praise in no small-scale,

always be thankful and gracious,
but remember, don't you ever inhale.

We Will Rejoice!

When all is said and done,
our religion is a joyful one!

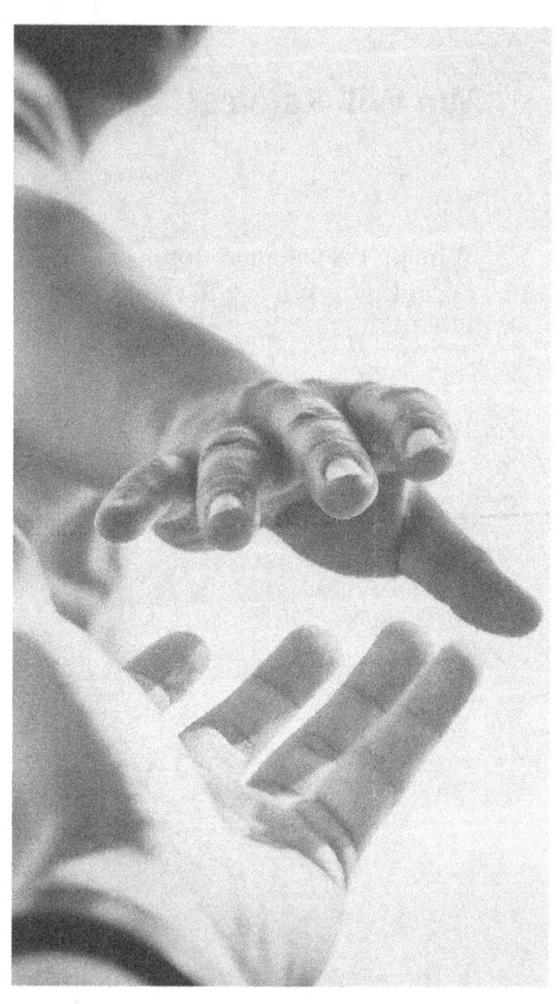

The Greatest Calling

*"The most important calling... is the one
you currently have."*

This simple command:
Lift where you stand!

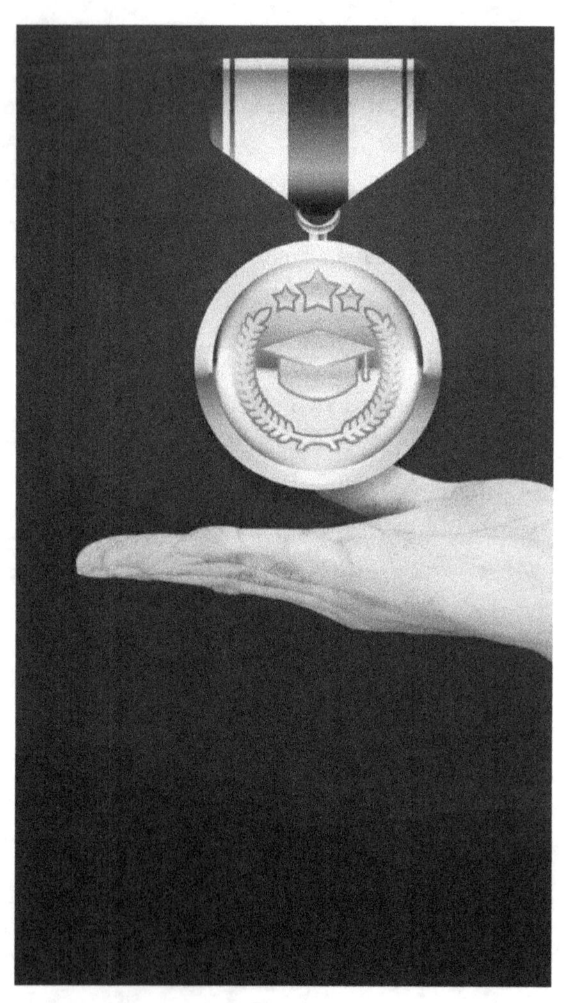

Without Fanfare

No matter what
you feel you deserve,

God's greatest reward
goes to those who serve

without
expectation of reward.

Out of Small Things

Blessings come,
His voice says,

not because of your abilities
but because of your choices.

BLESSINGS

Glory and Grandeur

The blessings of
the priesthood transcend

our ability to
even comprehend.

His Peace

The fires and tumults
of mortal life
may threaten and frighten
and never cease,

but those who incline
their hearts toward God
will be encircled
by His loving peace.

Not Forever

The pain and sorrow
you experience and see

is not what
forever will be.

Save Your Marriage!

To save your marriage
from destroying powers,
pull out the weeds
and water the flowers.

I hope you have enjoyed this little volume.

Please post an honest 5-star review on any book site where you have an account and posting privileges. Maybe you can mention which Latter-day Grook was your favorite.

If you found this book enjoyable, inspirational, educational, or enlightening, please tell your friends about it.

About the Author

Bill Wylson is the author of over 50 published writings on family values, religious issues, and religious education. His work has appeared in *The Ensign, This People, The New Era, Liberty Magazine, Success,* and others.

Bill graduated as a commercial copywriter from the *Columbia School of Broadcasting* in Hollywood, CA. He wrote trade journal ads for a major advertising agency in Los Angeles and public service announcements for a Los Angeles television station.

He has served as a volunteer Board Member of *Advocates of Single Parent Youth, Special Fun Games for the Disabled*, and on the Boards of Arts and Theater Councils. He has also served on Advisory Committees for the *Volunteer Center of Los Angeles* and on the *United Way Government Affairs Committee.*

Bill Wylson lives in South Jordan, Utah.

Other Books by Bill Wylson

Give Place in Your Heart:
31 Promises from the Book of Mormon

We are all familiar with Moroni's promise that Christ will manifest the truth of the Book of Mormon to us by the power of the Holy Ghost. This is just one of many promises the Lord has made regarding the Book of Mormon.

In *Give Place in Your Heart*, Bill Wylson outlines 31 promises, with their attendant blessings and conditions, that the Lord would love to bestow upon you.

Climate change is real.

There really should be no question about it. However, polarized views about climate issues stretch from the causes and cures for climate change to issues of trust or skepticism in climate scientists and their research.

According to NASA: *"Climate change is one of the most complex issues facing us today. It involves many dimensions—science, economics, society, politics, and moral and ethical questions—and is a global problem, felt on local scales, that will be around for decades and centuries to come."*

The only real question is: "What can we do about it?"

The answer might surprise you.

Grooks
Volumes One and Two

Grooks were created by the Danish poet Piet Hein (1905–1996), who wrote over 10,000 of them in Danish and English. A grook ('gruk' in Danish) is a form of short aphoristic poem or rhyming aphorism.

Literary experts suggest that the term 'gruk' is a compilation of the Danish words 'GRin and sUK', meaning to laugh and sigh. Grooks are multifaceted and intended to be spirit-building. They are often characterized by irony, paradox, brevity, precise use of language, rhythm, and rhyme.

In these volumes, Bill Wylson has attempted to cite the words and teachings of modern-day prophets and apostles from the Church of Jesus Christ of Latter-day Saints and to express their ideas in the form of latter-day grooks.

Three Minutes Eighteen Seconds:
A Prophet's Final Message to the World

Words are extremely powerful. Lord Byron poetically portrays this truth:

"But words are things, and a small drop of ink,
Falling like dew, upon a thought, produces
That which makes thousands, perhaps millions, think."

Three Minutes Eighteen Seconds examines three "small drops of ink" that simultaneously are extremely powerful words spoken by President Thomas S. Monson at the April 2017 General Conference, his final message to the people of this world.

Hieroglyphs, Golden Plates and Typos:

On the inside cover of his first leather-bound Book of Mormon, my father had written the following quotation from the prophet Joseph Smith:

"I told the brethren that the Book of Mormon was the most correct of any book on earth, and the keystone of our religion, and a man would get nearer to God by abiding by its precepts, than by any other book."

Directly below this quote, my father had compiled a list of scriptures labeled: "Mistakes in the Book of Mormon."

Committing his writings to the future reader, Moroni candidly and apologetically acknowledged: *"And if there be faults, they be the faults of a man. But behold, we know no fault."* How did my father have the audacity to make a list of mistakes in the Book of Mormon? To better understand these 'corrections' in the Book of Mormon and how they testify to its truthfulness and authenticity, we need to understand the process involved in making plates of ore and the method for inscribing on them.

Elder Hammond and the Inspector

"There's a word to describe someone who won't even bother to meet you at the bus station. It starts with an 'O' or, I don't know, maybe a 'C' or something. I think it's C-a—. No, I've lost it."

Elder Hammond was a freckled-face, shy sort of bumpkin from some rural farm town in Kansas. He was awkward and withdrawn. Even in his white shirt and tie, he reminded you of the type of kid you'd see in denim coveralls, wearin' a straw hat and chompin' on a thin blade of grass whilst irrigatin' the lower forty.

I knew nothing about Elder Hammond's personal life. He was just a simple, quiet, humble boy, determined and dedicated. He had no delusions of grandeur, just a desire to serve. Perhaps more than any missionary, Elder Hammond had a purity of spirit and an altruistic motivation in ministering. I pitied him. I think he actually believed he could make a difference.

The Manger on the Mantle
A Christmas Tale Based on Two True
Stories

The Manger on the Mantle recounts the tragic life of Mark Spencer, a man raised in a small town who somehow becomes very lost in the massive city of Los Angeles. He doesn't become geographically lost; he becomes spiritually lost.

Mark realizes how tainted his life has become as his family falls apart and his world collapses. He has strayed so far from the innocence of his youth, and now he fears he may never find his way back.

That's when Mark meets Marvin, a sockless, root-beer-float-toting ex-hippie. Together, they journey the road to Bethlehem as they ponder the purpose of a birth in a lowly manger.

The Manger on the Mantle is a beautiful story of hope, redemption, and the joyous possibility of being given a second chance.

The Greatest Thing in the World
The Restored Gospel Version

In 1883, Scottish scientist-evangelist Henry Drummond presented a powerful essay on 1 Corinthians 13, Paul's chapter on charity, the pure love of Christ. The "Restored Gospel Version" adds the perspective of modern-day revelation to a timeless classic.

Drummond's message of charity is as vital and essential today as when he first delivered it: *"The words which all of us shall one day hear sound not of theology, but of life, not of churches and saints but of the hungry and the poor, not of creeds and doctrines, but of shelter and clothing, not of Bibles and prayerbooks but of cups of cold water offered in the name of Christ."*

The essay has three parts: the contrast, the analysis, and The Defense. Drummond's simple yet profound message is short, but it can and should alter your life. The Reverend Dwight Moody said he had *"never heard anything so beautiful."*

The Greatest Thing in the World is a book that belongs in everyone's library.

References

The Great Commandment	GC October 2009
Try (And keep on Trying)	Internet Quote
Gratitude	GC April 2014
A Step Forward	GC October 2020
No Respecter of Persons	GC October 2017
It Matters Not	GC April 2016
God Calls to You	GC October 2017
Listen	GC October 2017
Start Where You Are	GC October 2015
Stand Loyal	GC October 2015
A Tribute to Joseph	GC October 2020
One Simple Fact	GC October 2015
Curing Weltschmerz	GC October 2018
Nearer My God to Thee	GC October 2020
What Hope?	GC October 2014
Draw Near to God	GC October 2018
This Very Day and Always	GC October 2014
Testimony of His Power	GC October 2020
Awaken	GC April 2014
The Words of the Prophets	GC October 2013
Turn Your Heart	GC October 2013
Footnote	GC April 2012
Endless Compassion	GC October 2018
A Paradox of Man:	GC October 2011
Our Part	GC October 2020
Eternal Repercussions	GC April 2016
Charity's Great Enemy	GC April 2016
Imperfect People	GC October 2018
The First Shall Be Last	GC October 2011
Distractions	GC April 2009
Day of Judgment	GC October 2016
Lessons in Adversity	GC October 2009
Regardless	GC October 2018
Take Up Thy Bed, and Walk	GC October 2017
Learn	GC October 2009